First published in Great Britain in 1994
This edition first published in 1999 by Dean
an imprint of Egmont Children's Books Limited
a division of Egmont Holding Limited
239 Kensington High Street, London W8 6SA

ISBN 0 603 55984 0

3 5 7 9 10 8 6 4 2

A CIP catalogue record for this book is available at the British Library

Printed in Hong Kong

Postman Pat's

"One, two, three,
Count with me."
Can you count with Postman Pat?

1 •

2 ••

3

4

5

6

7

8

9

10

Postman Pat has one cat called Jess.

two

There are two wheels on Miss Hubbard's bicycle.

three

Charlie Pringle has three books from the library.

4

four

There are four sheep crossing the road.

five

Pat buys five bananas from Sam Waldron's shop.

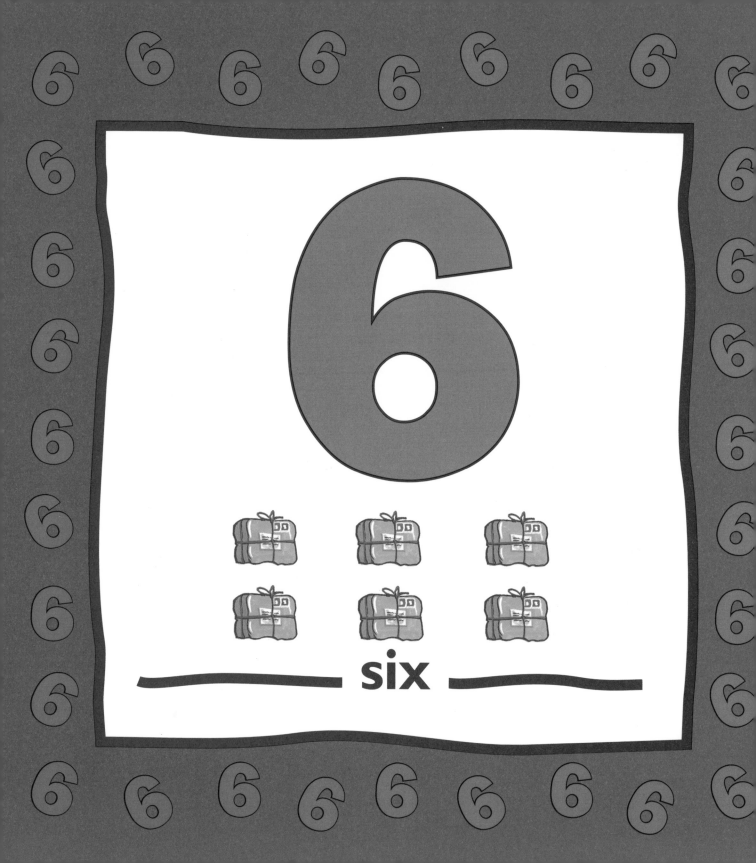

6

six

Pat has six parcels to deliver.

7

seven

There are seven chickens at Greendale Farm.

8

eight

Katy and Tom Pottage have eight marbles.

9

nine

Dorothy Thompson has nine tulips in her garden.

10

ten

Mrs Goggins has ten letters for Pat to deliver.

Postman Pat has gone home to have tea with his family.

How many teapots can you see on the table?
How many cups and saucers?
How many sandwiches?

Jess is having a bowl of milk.
"Miaow," he says.

Goodnight.